Manderstanding

Learn How to Read the Cues and Understand the Motives of the Male Gender

By Landon T. Smith

I0413839

Table of Contents

Introduction

"Men," you might say with a roll of your eyes as you witness a group of hyper masculine bro's high five. Perhaps your husband has forgotten an anniversary again or maybe you're stuck dealing with his immaturity for the 40th time this month. Indeed, it might seem from the outside, that men are completely clueless, irrational, emotionless or even stupid. Yet, is that really true? Does the masculine mind truly operate in such simplistic terms?

We live in an era where equality has rapidly made strides. Women have steadily been rising up through the ranks and the traditional stigma of being a woman has mainly gone by the wayside. There are still areas of resistance and prejudices, of course, but thanks to feminism, the female worker has more power than ever.

Yet, as women continue to ascend to power and are no longer bound by their gender, many of them are noticing a sharp contrast in the men that they work with. These men are hard to understand, their motives are confusing and worst of all, it seems from the outset that their actions are highly inconsistent with their personality types. You might be someone who finds herself mystified by why men act the way they do. The more that a woman has to work with men, the more she might be confused by their reasoning skills or decision making processes. However are you supposed to get ahead in the workplace without an understanding of the male psyche?

Fortunately, with Manderstanding, we are here to help illuminate the mental processes that go on through a man's mind. We will talk about the formation of the male psyche, how he relates to others, what is really happening in his mind and how you can learn to interact with men on their level. The majority of communication problems in this world stem from a lack of understanding the other person. Once you have a clear understanding of what motivates and drives men forward, you will be far better off in your workplace, relationships, friendships and even with things such as negotiation!

Be cautioned, however, if you are looking for a simplistic portrait of masculinity, if you are expecting to read about how the majority of men are sex-driven and primarily derive satisfaction from being dominant, you are in for a real surprise. The heart of a man is not driven by his need for sex, nor his need for control, but rather for his need for purpose. Let's move onto the first chapter to see what happens during the first phase of masculine development: boyhood.

Chapter 1: A Father and Son

To truly be able to understand the male motivation, we must be able to understand how they developed. In order to do so, we must look at the formative years of a male child. There are essentially three phases that every man must go through, boyhood, adolescence and manhood. The first two phases are based around physical and sexual development. The last phase, manhood, however, is not a physical or sexual development, but rather it is largely a piece of mental development. But before we delve into the final phase, let's look at what boyhood means.

Men are geared to be different than women in a variety of ways. The first is that men were primarily created with the purpose of being the hunter, the fighter, the warrior and the soldier. If we look at just about every society in the world, it is clearly seen that the men are expected to take up the burden of violence. They hunt, kill, fight and endure a great amount of suffering so that the tribe or civilization is able to thrive. On a physiological level, this means that men's bodies tend to have higher levels of upper body strength, a great amount of testosterone and brains that are geared to focus on one thing at a time. This allows them to have unparalleled combat and focusing abilities in times of great stress.

In our modern-day era, the race for equality has unfortunately led to some causalities. One such casualty is the ability to say that there is a difference between men and women. No matter how hard we try to reach a point where both sexes are treated equally, there will never be a way around it: men and women are physically different and it is a vast difference. The physical differences are not only in characteristics and sexual organs, but also in the way that our brains our wired. The problem isn't that men and women are different, traditionally the problem has been that one set of characteristics have been treated as *better* than the other set of characteristics. So, as we look at the masculine development process, we must be willing to accept that men are at a core level *different from women in both physical and mental development.* For many people this can be a no-brainer, but it's worth mentioning due to the politicization of gender that has happened in the last few years.

So, with the understanding that the masculine body is designed to function within a hunting, fighting and combat capacity, we must then look at what boyhood for a traditional hunter-gatherer tribe would look like. When a boy is born, he is primarily reared by his mother, but he will reach a point in his development when he, for the good of the tribe or civilization, must depart from his mother's side and learn primarily from his father. Each generation is entirely dependent on their parents to endow them with an understanding of the world, morality, and survival skills if they are going to be successful. Each gender has skills that must be imparted to their next of kin. A mother must pass her skills in motherhood in order for her daughter to be a successful mother herself. A father must pass on his skills in fatherhood if he wants his son to be a successful man.

This is the natural order of how we grow up. We are taught and trained by those who have given life to us. As the boy grows up, he is taught a great many things about what his responsibilities are. He is taught how to fight, how to be strong, how to bear great burdens and how to be a leader. He is not simply taught through words, but also in action. The father doesn't sit and tell the boy all about hunting, but rather the father takes the boy out and shows him how. Eventually the boy is expected to hunt on his own. He grows strong and capable in the world around him, all thanks to his father's tutelage. This leads him to transition from his adolescent phase into his manhood phase. Only when a man is strong, confident and capable of mastering the environment around him does he truly feel like a man.

This system is integral for the development of the masculine mind. A boy, simply put, must have a father who is willing to rear him and transfer all of his life skills onto his son. This is a crucial step that will lead to a functional member of society at the end. However, as civilization has advanced and society has grown more complicated, the father role has begun to diminish significantly. This is caused by a few effects. The first is that formalized education has replaced the need for a one on one style of education, in which the father would pass his skills onto his son. The son now needs to go to school and receive an education in order to function in society. His doesn't learn his skills from his father, but rather gains credentials from a university or a college where is able to determine his own career. The second reason why the father's role has diminished is that the nuclear family has been severely disrupted in most family lineages. Either a divorce, death or emotional abandonment has caused a great deal of men to grow up without fathers or worse, fathers who were physically present but emotionally absent.

Since each generation learns everything that they need to function from the generation behind them, if there is a break in the chain, the effects can be devastating. When a father isn't present or able to impart values and wisdom into his son, the son grows up without having the necessary skills to pass down to his children. All it takes is for one break in the chain and things go all haywire. Each generation it will get worse and worse until we see a total degradation in male culture.

A boy in the modern-day world has a very real chance of growing up without a father, or with a father who grew up without being taught all of the things necessary to be a real man. This means that there is an increasing number of men who are coming into this world who are moving through boyhood and adolescence, but aren't able to sufficiently transition into the stage of manhood as quickly as their sexual characteristics mature. In other words, a boy doesn't fully grow up just because his body is 21. The mental and physical maturity of a man are usually very different from each other.

On the other hand, when it comes to females, they tend to mature a lot faster than men do in both the physical and emotional realm. A man's brain hasn't fully matured until he hits the age of 27 or 28, as opposed to the female brain that matures relatively early on during adolescence. This creates a significant gap in the way that both genders learn and can lead to the picture that men are somewhat less complex than women. The reality is that men aren't less complicated than women, they just develop much differently.

The digital world has removed a lot of the primitive functionality of masculinity, whereas the new era has only opened up to *more* opportunities for women. A boy growing up today will most likely never have to hunt in order to survive, fight against a fierce beast to protect the tribe or join a raiding party against his enemies, but a woman still faces a lot of the common experiences that defined womanhood several thousand years back. She still has the ability to raise children, to nurture, to take care of others, and with the advent of feminism, she can also fulfill a lot of functions that had traditionally been reserved for the male. Hunting has been replaced with working a job that pays money. Defending a tribe has been replaced with paying taxes so the police can keep an eye on things. The role of protector, defender and ruler is no longer a matter of strength, but rather it is a matter of specialization.

This has created a major anxiety in the modern-day boy. His naturally physical and violent urges are curbed, he is scolded for his rambunctiousness and instead of being allowed to explore the wild world around him, he's shoved in a desk where he must be still and quiet for 8 hours a day. He learns to that his natural desire to make noise, be strong and brave, must be suppressed due to the existence of politeness. There are designated times where he is allowed to make noise and run around, but for the most part, he is controlled.

At home, he grows distracted by movies and video games, things that allow him to experience what his most natural and primal desires are through a safe medium. He finds fulfillment and value in these things. If he doesn't have a father present, or a father willing to invest in him, this boy will end up growing up without a strong understanding of who he is.

Then, he reaches an age where he is 18. He is registered to be in the Selective Services and told that he is now a man. People tell him to man up when he's not acting responsibly. The sitcoms and the televisions tell him that being a man means to be obsessed with sex and beer. His ability to form relationships with other men tend to be cautious and shallow, because he hasn't learned how to relate on a deeper level. In essence, a boy grows up in a world that is no longer suited to him.

Many women might find this hard to believe due to the fact that the world is dominated by men still. The sexism and misogyny still exists and a great deal of workplaces can be perceived as a boy's club. Let's be real here, men are still the dominant members of society, but that is not because of how they grew up, but rather the core desire that drives them forward no matter what. In the next chapter, we'll look at what a man's real desire is and how it shapes his entire action. The takeaway from this chapter is that boys aren't growing up as quickly as they used to, primarily because the modern era has taken away a lot of his rites of passage. This is the reason we tend to see so many young men who live their lives as if they were still teenagers, despite the fact that they are fully grown adults.

Chapter 2: The Heart of a Man

An old adage is that women care about love and men only care about sex. This is a frequent picture of what drives the male psyche in films and television shows. Pop-psychology often tells women different ways to use sex as a way to make a man feel like he is a man. There are millions of pornographic websites out there designed to entice and scintillate men. All of these things exist on a flawed assumption. The assumption is that sex is the core desire of a man. Truthfully, a man desires something far more than just sexual connection.

Sex is a physiological need for men. Their bodies are designed to impregnate women indiscriminately and with very little need for preparation. The male body has strong hormones that urge him on to reproduce, but we must also acknowledge that unlike women, who have a specific timer on their reproductive abilities, the male body stays pretty much virile for his entire life. This means that the sex drive will almost always be present in his life. Despite how strong the sex drive is in a man, it does wax and wane depending on what he is focusing on, what his testosterone level is and his emotional securities.

While men might always be perceived to be ready to have sex, the truth is that their willingness directly corresponds to their arousal levels. When a male is in a high level of arousal, the sex drive grows stronger and he becomes far more interested in achieving release. However, if he has no arousal nor any stimulus that leads to arousal, he is able to function normally. Sex will not come into the equation *as a physiological motivator*. This is important to distinguish.

The truth is that most men's intense desire for sex isn't based off of their physiologies need to procreate, but rather it's based off of the validation that they receive from sex. In other words, men don't use sex to fulfill their need for sex, but rather men use sex to fulfill some other need. And what is that need? That need is the core drive that is deep within every man's heart, it is the need to *matter*.

Men are born with an inherent desire to shape the world around them. They were created to tame a wild world and fight against the forces of chaos. Their hearts are extremely focused on the experience of achievement. They want to achieve great things. They want to know that they are capable of getting things done. This is the purest desire in a man's heart. His satisfaction comes from climbing mountains, creating beautiful works of art, winning a fistfight or discovering a new cure to a disease.

The male heart is one that is center around motion, action and achievement. This is the lens and filter that he will experience everything through. So, when he is able to have sex with a woman, he is, in a way, experiencing a conquest. When a man experiences the thrill of victory, it releases endorphins within him, it fulfills a function that he was created to desire and it motivates him to do more. This is why we often see successful men reaching success at a large amount of things. Each time they are able to achieve some level of success, it gives them a hunger for more and they continue onward.

To contrast the male motivation with female motivation, women traditionally tend to have a less action oriented approach to life. Their central desires are based around connection, intimacy and to be heard. A woman would look at a home and wonder how she can fill it full of people who will make her happy, a man will look at a home and wonder what he can do to improve the home itself.

These are rough sketches of motivation, of course. Every person is different and there are a great deal of men and women who have desires that are atypical of their gender. But for the majority of the population, most men are going to be process and task oriented. This is a crucial thing to understand, because once you have a knowledge of what drives and motivates a man, you can then begin to make sense of the decisions that he makes.

So, the masculine desire is essentially about achievement, but how conscious is this desire? Unfortunately, the way the society has continued to advance, the desire isn't particularly understood by the men themselves. Their restlessness, their desire for more tends to be preyed upon through systems that create feelings of achievement within them. For example, video games and sports on television can help a man feel as if he is accomplishing something by allowing him to vicariously live through other people or experiences. When a gamer is fighting against a monster, his brain is releasing dopamine, the same chemical that releases whenever a man were to achieve any major accomplishment.

Since the modern era has the power to release dopamine through things such as entertainment, drugs, alcohol and sex, most men find that they are attracted to these things on a greater level. When a man begins to watch his favorite movie, he doesn't just witness a story happening, he begins to simulate it in his mind. He experiences a phantom type of satisfaction, the kind that doesn't involve any real accomplishment, but lets him temporarily feel as if he were getting something done. This in turn creates a greater hunger to consume more of the media.

Of course, we are not decrying any form of entertainment here, but most women who struggle with significant others who are overly absorbed into their preferred choice of entertainment usually don't understand why connection is so difficult for men. The reality is that connection doesn't particularly have an end goal. Men prefer to think in compartmentalized squares and prefer to handle things one at a time. More than anything, they tend to be goal oriented and driven toward solving problems in a series of steps. Relational things such as communication are also approached that way.

If the heart of a man is built around the idea that he must achieve in order to feel valuable and worthy, what is he to do in a world where there isn't much for him to achieve? Perhaps he isn't well educated, maybe hasn't been given the proper tools to achieve success on a professional level. Regardless of the reason that he feels like his accomplishments are stunted, he will begin to find other ways to reach the feeling of accomplishment, as stated before. This often leads to the corruption of the masculine energy, which usually results in a wide variety of inappropriate or selfish behaviors. Let's move on to the next chapter where we will examine the different archetypes of men who have begun to focus on a specific type of accomplishment in order to receive satisfaction.

Chapter 3: The Corrupt Male Energy

As we've seen, masculinity is intensely focused on achievement and a great deal of male energy goes toward reaching some level of importance in their lives. Where they often fall short is in the fact that *feeling* important is readily available in this society, due to a wide variety of abuses. Men can quickly fall into several different types of cycles, where they begin to experience something that makes them feel as if they are valid and important, but those sources are often dubious in nature. When the male energy begins to focus on the experiences that provide validation exclusively, those energies become corrupt. Let's look at a list of different types of corrupted male energies through what would be known as an archetype.

Archetype One: The Approval Hound

The approval hound is the type of guy who is desperately looking for approval from other people. He is willing to do just about anything in order to receive a "good job" from his boss, wife, mother or neighbor. In general, there can be a healthy amount of looking for approval, but when it comes to the approval hound, he goes way overboard. The problem is that his desire for approval, for receiving pleasure from making other people happy, will override every other desire in his life.

This is where yes men come from. They can be approval hounds who will do whatever it takes to make their boss or wife happy, not because they are weak willed, but because of the dopamine rush they receive when they have done a good job. Approval hounds make for excellent workers, but in relationships you might find them to be very frustrating because of their willingness to ditch current plans in favor of what other people have in store for them. This might play out like your husband cancelling a weekend getaway because he has to go into work, or it might look like a boyfriend who has to stay late at work every single night.

The problem with dealing with approval hounds is that since they are primarily driven by their need to hear good job, they are extremely easy to stretch thin. They might end up agreeing to fifteen different commitments, fully knowing that they aren't able to meet any of them in a timely manner. Yet the pleasure of coming through, of getting things done, might drive them to be hyper-functional individuals. Men who are skilled at getting a lot of things done in a short amount of time are usually approval hounds. At the same time, they might also end up being perceived as unreliable or lazy due to the fact that they said yes to something they can't reasonably do.

It's important to be able to look past a man's words and instead focus on his deeds. If you see that he is pushing too hard toward gaining approval of those who are superior, you can be sure that he is primarily motivated by approval. The solution to dealing with this kind of man isn't to try and give him the most approval, so that you can win him over, but rather to work to show him what actually motivates him. Most approval hounds don't really realize it, they just think they are overly busy or hyper competent. Some of them have emotional trouble saying no because they fear losing approval. By being able to point out that his internal value has nothing to do with what other people think, you will be able to assist an approval hound in finding out there are more important things in life to worry about. Of course, you must be cautious in dealing with an approval hound when you try to help them change, primarily because they most likely will try to change in such a way that will please you. This will only last temporarily of course, so make sure that you don't believe their initial change. It will take quite some time for an approval hound to be able to learn how to seek their own approval before they seek the approval of others.

Just make sure that you aren't someone who's adding fuel to the fire by taking advantage of them in this state. It's far better to have a relationship with a man who's free from the need of approval from others than to use his own approval seeking ways to further your own goals.

Archetype Two: The Escapist

The Escapist is the type of guy who, upon getting home from work, immediately goes to his computer or television and unplugs from reality for quite some time. Maybe he spends upwards to several hours a day playing a video game, maybe he watches a lot of sports, either way, he's spending a lot of time away from reality and this can put a strain on your relationship. It might be frustrating to have to feel like you are somehow competing with electronics or some hobby for your man's affections. From the outside, it might seem like what drives the escapist is pure selfishness, an overwhelming desire to get what he wants and ignore the needs of others in order to get it.

The reality is that the escapist isn't acting upon any selfish desire, but rather he is reacting so that he can protect himself from the stresses and pains of his everyday life. His focus isn't on himself, but rather on getting away from everything, including himself. This is why it is so easy for an escapist to completely lose track of time and neglect his own health and personal appearance. His mindset is entirely engaged on getting away that he doesn't pay any attention to the present.

Yet, from the outside it may appear that the escapist is simply interested in his own hobby past the point of healthiness. From a relationship standpoint, it is almost impossible to understand the draw to play video games or watch television to that degree, unless you are willing to learn what is going on beneath the surface in the mind of the escapist.

The escapist's mind is full of doubt, anxiety and fear. Instead of dealing with those emotions in a positive, healthy manner, he has instead chosen to find an unhealthy way to ignore those feelings. Therefore, we can conclude that a man who is seeking out refuge in drugs, alcohol, sports or gaming is actually an emotionally stunted individual who is unable to handle their own feelings properly. The root cause of this escapism most likely comes from the fact that at some point in their developmental process, they were introduced to something that satisfied their needs enough to where they didn't have to worry about their emotional problems. Without being taught how to manage his own emotions, the escapist most likely will suppress his feelings unconsciously.

Therefore, when dealing with an escapist male, it is important to not look at the hobby or activity as the problem, because in reality, it is merely a *symptom*. Millions of people watch television, sports, play video games or indulge in hobbies without being completely absorbed by them. If we cast blame on the escape, we are ignoring what the escapist is hiding from. He isn't hiding from work, he isn't hiding from his responsibilities and he's not hiding from you, in reality, he is hiding from his own emotions. He doesn't know how to handle them, so he's learned methods of suppressing them, the strongest is to crank up the dopamine by playing a video game, getting high or watching movies endlessly.

Of course, women tend to be a little less emotionally suppressive than men do. Men are often stereotyped as being unemotional, but that is because the male culture has created a world where it is considered to be "girly" or "gay" to express emotions other than anger. Things like sorrow are hidden away, for fear of being mocked or called weak. Therefore, when a woman is in a relationship with an escapist and she sees him vegging out every single night, catatonic before a flickering screen, her initial reaction isn't to see that there is an emotional struggle going on within his heart, but rather her reaction is to feel ignored and frustrated by him. The truth is that if he were emotionally healthy, he wouldn't be ignoring his wife or girlfriend in the least.

It is easy to be insensitive to this situation and look at yourself as the primary victim. After all, since you are being ignored, aren't you the one who has the right to anger? Truthfully, has anger ever solved the problem? When you react with anger, hostility or judgment, all you do is create more emotional tension within the escapist, causing him to dig further into his own hole. The more you pull, the harder he will dig into his own position. Therefore, it would be a far better solution to not react to his escapist tendencies and instead try to focus on learning how to draw him out to talk about his problems.

Men have classically been trained to ignore their own feelings and treat them as if they weren't really there. They hide from their emotions and it rots within them. Women have a better handle on their emotions (despite what culture says) primarily because they are used to actively experiencing them and acknowledging them. When strong emotions arrive, they will stay for a while and then leave of their own volition. However, when you try to suppress them, they end up sticking around far longer than you would want.

So how do you deal with the escapist? It's not easy, but it requires patience, love and a willingness to help him express what is actually bothering him. Don't necessarily aim for fixing him, but rather try to encourage him to talk about his day, his thoughts and his feelings. It would be a bad idea to try and intercept his time in front of the television or the computer, so make sure that you are able to communicate to him before or after his escape time. Eventually, the more you are able to draw things out of him, the more he will be able to acknowledge his own feelings and feel less pressure to hide from them.

Archetype Three: The Victim

Perhaps one of the more frustrating archetypes to handle when dealing with men, the victim is the type of person who is unable to take responsibility for his actions and instead looks to others to clean up after him. He is either oversensitive, lazy or easily provoked into anger. The victim is the kind of guy who looks for any excuse to make things about him. If he's cut off in traffic, he'll grow angry because how dare they treat *him* that way? If he doesn't get a promotion, he'll cry and fuss about how he deserved better but was treated poorly for some reason or another. The victim is an interesting archetype of corrupt male energies because as our society continues to advance, there are far more men who are fitting this mold.

The victim mindset comes from a need for a recognition, without a clear understanding that work is required to get that. In other words, the victim is an extremely entitled person who thinks that they are *owed* something in this life. Every interaction is looked at through this lens of entitlement. Therefore, when the victim is denied something, hurt unintentionally, or otherwise bothered, he will take a position of being wounded. This wounded position will require others to give him sympathy or what he wants, allowing for him to advance in society.

This might seem like it is directly in contradiction to the male achievement drive that pretty much leads all men forward, but it is, in fact, directly tied to the male desire for achievement. The victim wants to achieve things just as much as a healthily functioning man, but he lacks the ability to do so by hard work because he doesn't have the ethic or the inclination. So, as a way to cope for this, he has learned that a specific type of behavior will provide him with the same level of satisfaction as achievement. So, when he loses the sports contest, he'll fuss about the other person cheating as opposed to accepting that he failed and moving on, solely because he desires to experience satisfaction. By being the victim, in some twisted way, he is able to experience a pseudo-satisfaction that doesn't require him to work at all.

Being in a relationship with a victim type man is difficult because you will really, truly believe that life is difficult for him. The stories he tells will always involve some kind of injustice, the excuses that he has puts him at dead last in the race of life and you will tend to experience a higher level of sympathy for him. Then, you might find yourself doing favors for him, trying to cheer him up, putting energy into helping him get to where he says he wants to be. However, you'll find later that for some reason, all of the energy that you've put into him just seems to fall flat. He doesn't improve, he doesn't look for a job, he doesn't improve the relationships that are bringing him down.

The reality is that when you are in a relationship with the victim type of man, he is going to allow you to focus as much energy as you like on making him feel better, but won't try to improve things on his own because he truthfully doesn't want to improve. There is a lot of hard work that is required to improve your life and you have to be willing to spend a long time and a great deal of effort if you want success. Someone who is always pointing at external things as the reason for his failures is someone who is incapable of achieving real success. Instead, they have found a suitable replacement for success: being the victim. As long as they get attention, special treatment and love for their behavior, they will continue to do so.

The solution for handling a professional victim is fairly simple. Stop coddling them and stop giving into their behavior. It's easy for them to pretend like they are in a serious state of emotional disrepair, but you will be able to know better once you start looking at how they never really seem to want to improve. Don't indulge them in their inappropriate behavior and you will find that they will grow more frustrated and hostile with you. The victim position is more or less an act they have adopted in order to gain sustenance, hopefully by starving them of your sympathy, you can help inspire them to move forward. If they try to grow more dramatic about their desire for validation through things such as threats or accusations of your lack of love, don't feel bad about cutting the cord. A victim needs to hit rock bottom before they realize how their behavior is actually sabotaging them from real success. Only when they are completely alone and unable to gain satisfaction from sympathy will they actually change. A willingness to stick around is nothing more than pure enablement. Don't allow a victim to manipulate you into thinking that they need you, you aren't their mother.

Archetype Four: The Overcompensator

The Overcompensator is the kind of guy who is overly aggressive or macho. He's the kind of guy who drives a loud truck, is always getting into fights at bars or tries to brag about how much money he makes. The Overcompensator, from the outside, seems to be brave, strong and proud. He seems like he has the greatest amount of confidence in the world and that life is going well for him. Relationally, however, you might not particularly care for him. His aggression, his bravado and outspokenness might put you at odds. In fights, you might end up feeling overwhelmed by his desire to get the last word in or even his physical stance.

The truth about overcompensators is that they are just nothing more than posers who have learned that a certain pattern of behavior can hide them from their insecurities. A man who is overly aggressive, acts like he has a chip on his shoulder and treats people with disrespect most likely experiences a deep feeling of fear. He developed this pattern of behavior as a means of protecting himself from various emotional threats. You would assume that the

Overcompensator isn't particularly an emotional person, but that couldn't be farther from the truth. The Overcompensator is an extremely emotional person, he just channels all of his fears into things such as anger or rage.

Anger is a powerful drug, it gives a person a sense of control. A man's anger gives him a rush of endorphins that makes him feel as if he were able to take hold of just about any situation and win. The male body is designed to fight and as such, when anger and aggression is rushing through him, he will feel far more confident in himself. However, we must be willing to ask the question: where does anger come from? A lot of people make the assumption that anger exists entirely by itself, but truthfully, anger is a secondary emotion. Anger comes entirely from fear. When a person is scared, one physiological response is to get angry, as a means of protecting yourself. For example, if a man were coming to kill another man with a knife, the victim of the attack would become angry. The anger would allow him to defend himself and fight back against the assailant.

Anger exists as a means to protect, but only comes into existence when a person is scared. So, when we see men who are big, brash and prone to anger, it is very likely that in reality, their anger is coming from a sense of fear. And where does that fear come from? Usually, it comes from a feeling of inadequacy. They feel as if they aren't true men or that they aren't cut out for achieving greatness. These feelings make them afraid of who they really are and in the process, they seek a solution.

Overcompensators are easy to spot, because a great deal of men deal with these insecurities. They are desperate to call themselves men, because their fathers weren't able to help them transition into manhood and so they look at a list of traits and behaviors that are usually acceptable as "masculine." These traits include:

- Violence
- Aggression
- Disrespect towards women
- Wanting to be the Alpha Male
- Anger
- Hyper-sexuality

It is easy when you're in a relationship with an Overcompensator to believe that he is naturally that way. It's very easy to fall into trap of thinking that most men are like this or that this is a specific personality type of men. The truth is that it is nothing more than a stereotype created by popular depictions of what it means to be a man. If you watch sitcoms, read books and study the way modern culture depicts masculinity, you'll see the knuckle-dragging barbarian who is entirely out of touch with his own senses. Boys, growing up without strong father figures, look at these caricature's and then decides that they are supposed to be like them. Generations grow up believing that masculinity is defined by how many women a man can sleep with, how strong he is physically and how big his truck can be.

Is there an easy solution to dealing with an Overcompensator? Not particularly. These men are driven by a primal fear, a fear that will haunt them to no end. They might like to pretend that they are simplistic, but the Overcompensator is a deeply complex man who is hiding in his persona. When you can see past this façade, when you realize that the booming, howling man who's screaming at traffic is nothing more than a scared little boy, it will make it easier for you to be able to relate to him.

An overcompensator's anger issues can make it troublesome to have a relationship, primarily because our first instinct when anger presents itself towards us is to try and defend ourselves, meaning that we get angry back. However, once we realize that his anger stems from a deep-seated fear of the world around him, it helps us to remain calm even though he is mad at us. This allows us to keep our cool and solve the actual problem, instead of indulging in his anger and trying to fight back against him. Responding to anger or aggression with more anger only pours more gasoline on the fire. Instead, when you learn to respond with understanding and kindness, you'll be able to communicate far better with him.

All in all, these four archetypes make up a lot of what corrupted masculine energies can look like in this modern-day world. There are a lot of men out there who are picture perfect models of these archetypes primarily because of their desire for achievement. Not all men are like this, of course, but a great many are out there who meet these descriptions. Let's move onto the next section, where we shall begin to discuss how the male brain handles relationships.

Chapter 4: The Masculine Relationship

If we are to have a sufficient understanding of the male mind, we must be able to look at his relationships and the way that he relates to the people around him. A lot can be learned about a man by the way that he communicates and works with others. Being able to discern the logic behind his friendships will give you insight into what goes on in the core of his heart.

As stated before, men are highly driven by an achievement drive that pushes them to get things done. They were made for action, and as such, their energies when unrestricted go towards getting stuff taken care of. In the ancient days, the men were unified by a common goal: protect and advance the good of the tribe. They were men of action, and their friendships and relationships were all based around some kind of common goal. They weren't the types who would hang out and just talk about nothing, because in the ancient era there was no time to waste. Things needed to be done. It is from this core, the need to do action, that men form relationships.

There are several different types of male friendships and relationships that exist, some of them are older and more byzantine, others should be familiar to our modern culture. Let's look at each type of male relationship and explain what it looks like and what the effects of not having one looks like:

Relationship Type One: Father Figure

As you know, we have stressed the value of a father figure in the life of a man. The interesting thing about men is that if they are missing a father, they will naturally seek out some kind of father figure that will allow them to learn wisdom and experience. Depending on this person's surroundings and what access he has, he might find a father figure in a teacher, a pastor or a sports coach. This father figure will make a profound impact on them, one that will last for the rest of their life.

The absence of a father figure is immediately noticeable in the life of a man. You can see it in the way that they are unsure of themselves, or how they have become some kind of negative archetype. Not all men who don't have father figures turn out bad, but a great majority of them do suffer. The absence of a father figure will essentially rob them of their natural born desire to learn everything they can from an older, wiser figure.

Relationship Type Two: The Shallow Friend

Friendship is a curious ordeal for most men. They experience a great desire to be in community with their fellow men, but since they are naturally action oriented, their friendships often form around specific activities. This is why men so easily put together sporting groups, men's clubs, gaming groups, etc. They are unified entirely by their common interest. However, since there is an overwhelming focus on the actual activity itself, the male friendships tend to be very simplistic and shallow. A man could easily be part of a fishing group for several years and not know a single detail about his fellow fisherman other than what they caught last week.

There is a wide variety of reasons as to why men do not have deep relationships, nor people they could consider to be their best friends. The biggest reason is that unlike women, who are naturally more social, men have been conditioned by society to naturally be further apart. Society has created several false images of the idea that male friendship cannot be rugged, intense and personal without it being considered homosexual in nature. The word "bromance" is thrown around all the time, as a way to tease men who have especially close relationships with one another. All of this goes to create a pressure where men fear getting to close because they do not want to be perceived as gay. As society has grown more progressive over the last few years, we are seeing a greater amount of acceptance for those who are homosexual. This would indicate that perhaps men would stop being so worried about being perceived as gay and would be more secure in their own masculinity.

Another reason why male friendships tend to be shallow is because most men prefer to keep their private thoughts and emotions to themselves. Without having learned how to express themselves emotionally as children, due to pressures from school and parents, they will mostly keep to themselves. A real friendship can only grow when there is deep emotional connection, and if most men are hiding the emotional parts of themselves, there can hardly be a chance that they will be able to connect on that deeper level. Most men have experienced so shallow a friendship that they aren't even fully aware that a deeper kind of friendship can exist.

Relationship Type Three: Romantic

The romantic relationship is one of the few relationships where a man can fully express himself in pretty much every possible way. He is able to emotionally vulnerable without fear of judgment, his able to fulfill his sexual desires and he is able to tap into those primal emotions to protect and defend his significant other. The romantic relationship is one of the most important relationships to a man, and as we can see, a great deal of the world rotates around the idea of man pursuing after romance.

However, in the modern era, romance often translates straight to sex. Many women believe that men enjoy sex purely for the physical component, however, there is another layer to the sexual relationship for men that transcends the pleasure that comes from orgasm. This is the connection piece that most men unconsciously desire. Men deeply desire acceptance and one of the most powerful ways that a woman can accept a man is to allow him access to her body. This type of connection, this intimacy, can thrill him beyond anything that a simple sexual experience can. In fact, most men are always looking for this kind of connection because it is the most whole experience that they can have.

Of course, modern culture speaks very little of this. People often say, "it's just sex" but the romantic relationship is one of mystery and holds a very strong kind of power over a man. A man can make a seemingly unending series of poor decisions if he experiences sexual connection with a woman, as it fulfills the deeper longing in his own heart to achieve.

Relationship Type Four: The Deep Friendship

It is possible for a man to have deeper friendships in his life. In fact, without those deeper relationships, it is almost impossible for him to be able to thrive and accomplish greatness in his life. They aren't particularly common, but these kinds of friendships have usually endured a great deal of time in order to grow that way. A man who has a deep friendship has someone that he can always depend on in his time of need. The value of these deeper friendships doesn't undermine or supplant the romantic relationship, but can actually strengthen the romantic relationship primarily because when a man is experiencing great amounts of stress, he can look to his deep friendships to steer him down the right path.

Chapter 5: Masculinity and Respect

Men are naturally geared toward leadership. Their bodies and minds are geared toward taking action and as such, they have a natural tendency to lead. This isn't to say, of course, that all men are natural leaders, but the male heart has a great desire to be seen as someone who is strong, capable and above all, respectable. This is why many men run after positions of authority, because they often believe that a position of authority automatically carries with it an amount of respect.

Respect is extremely important for men, primarily because respect is a reflection of a person's opinion about him. When a man feels respected by his colleagues, he will naturally work for their good, but as soon as he realizes that he isn't respected by someone, he can grow frustrated and angry. Respect is based off of achievement. When you have respect for someone, it is because you are respecting their capabilities in some way. When a general is able to lead his troops through a battle with minimal casualties and win it, he earns respect. When a college professor publishes a brilliant article in the New York Times, he earns the respect of his fellow academics. Respect, at its core, is one of the most important parts in a man's life.

This is why he craves respect when it comes to leadership. If he is respected as a leader, he will feel strong and confident in his own abilities. Respect usually is a two-way street, he will give people respect and in turn, expect it back.

However, when a man consistently begins to experience a lack of respect, it can cause a great deal of frustration within the relationship. This can be a very common occurrence when it comes to fights between him and his significant other. While women do need to be respected, they are driven by the same level of achievement drive that men are. They don't naturally tie their own significance to what they can accomplish on this earth. Therefore, women don't necessarily feel a need for respect in the same way that a man does. A woman wants respect, in a lot of ways, a man needs respect. If he doesn't have respect in his relationships, it will create feelings of tension and insecurity. He will begin to doubt his value in the relationship and as such, react out of fear, anger and hostility.

This is why it's important for a woman to understand that even though she might not understand his decisions, when a man is taking a leadership position, it is important to be able to disagree with him without disrespecting him. Most men are perfectly willing to engage in disagreement, provided that they don't feel disrespected in the process. A simple disagreement can rapidly escalate into a serious conflict if a man feels disrespected. What are the ways that man feels disrespected? Let's take a look:

Tone:

Tone is extremely important when it comes to conveying respect to just about anyone. Men learned a long time ago, in the ancient era, that tone is extremely important when communicating with a potential enemy. Tone indicates whether there is danger or not, and it tells them whether they are being respected or not. When a tone indicates hostility, judgment or disappointment, it can easily convey to the man that he isn't being respected.

An emotional individual can easily fall into the trap of allowing their emotions to dictate their tone. A woman who is angry with a man's decision can begin to talk about her frustration in a logical manner, but if her tone indicates any kind of disrespect, it doesn't matter how logical her argument is, he will not really hear her words. He will hear "you are being disrespected" and it will cause his self-defensive mechanisms to kick in. For an Overcompensator, it will trigger an explosive episode, for the victim, it could cause crying.

This is one of the more unfortunate truths when it comes to learning how to communicate well with men, it doesn't mean a damn what your argument is. If your method of delivery has even a hint of a negative tone, it will tank the conversation almost immediately. You must be willing to keep your tone neutral or positive if you want to communicate with him. This will be a world of help when it comes to reaching resolution with problems or solving through disagreements amicably.

Ignoring Him:

Perhaps one of the most frustrating things that can lead to a man experiencing emotions of anger, rage and sorrow, is the feeling of being ignored by their significant other. This isn't to say that giving a man the silent treatment is frustrating, but rather it means that ignoring his council or just going ahead with your course of action without letting him get a say in the matter. This isn't about letting him control your actions, ultimately you have the freedom to choose whatever you wish, but it is important for a man to feel *heard* about matters that involve him as well. If he feels as if you don't consult him before you make serious decisions, then he will feel incredibly disrespected and that will lead to a greater sense of frustration and woundedness within him. A man doesn't always have to get his way in order to feel happy, but he does need to feel considered and respected. This can make all the difference when it comes to communication with a man.

Insults:

The idea that men are naturally tough and emotionless plays into a dangerous cultural problem: that it is permissible to insult a man. Most women feel like they can levy an insult at a man and that he'll get over it, but on the contrary, if you throw just the right insult at a man, it could wound him for years to come. The problem is that he will hide his wounded status and end up either angry or retreating. When a man is hurt, he usually tries to back away from the conversation, emotionally shutting down because he can't handle the surge of emotions that are coming to him. Instead of expressing those emotions healthily and functionally, he will instead opt to avoid dealing with the problem entirely. He will either depart from the situation entirely, or hide within his own manufactured persona.

The urge to insult can be extremely strong, but we must realize that when we insult a man during the course of a fight, it will serve nothing other than to disrespect him. This feeling of disrespect will remove any chance of the fight being a constructive one. Each time a man is insulted in a relationship, that wound will go down to his core and fester. He will carry it and since most men have very little ways to healthily express their pain, it will only do damage to him long term. It will push him deeper into his unhealthy patterns and this will ultimately lead to more arguments down the road.

There are certain types of insults that wound deeper than others. Here's a quick list for you to know to avoid saying at all costs:

His Earning Ability:

One of the greatest male insecurities is that they are expected to be the earners. Their ancient heritage in being the one to hunt, the one to bring back the meal for the tribe, has created a long-lasting desire to be the one who can provide. When a man is insulted in his ability to earn in a relationship, he will feel an intense, instinctual shame, despite the fact that we live in a modern era where relationships are considered to be equal. Part of the achievement drive is earning, and so an insult of this will quickly go to his core.

His Intelligence:

Targeting a man's intelligence plays upon his insecurities because intelligence is a comparative thing. When a man is being told "you aren't smart" or that "you're an idiot" what he really hears is "you aren't good enough for me." This can quickly go straight to his heart and since he doesn't have the ability to refute it with any kind of evidence or facts, primarily because the insult is an emotionally driven one and not a logical one, he will become very hurt.

He's Not Good Enough as Blank

Men are competitive. Their testosterone mixed with their leadership instincts means that most men are willing to get into fights over the smallest things. No man wants to come in last, instead, they all want to be in first place. So, when you tell a man that he isn't as good as your ex, your brother, his father, whomever, you are essentially taking all of the wind out of his sails.

Men want to compete, at a very innate level, so just handing the prize of First Place to some other guy can be a devastating experience for most men. He will grow frustrated with your words and as such, will either lash out or end up becoming far more submissive, in the hopes of earning your favor. Regardless, he will begin to resent not only you, but the other male that you have mentioned.

Indicating that you settled for him

If you're in a romantic relationship with him and you're in an argument, it might very tempting to levy the charge that you're regretful of your time with him. This can be devastating to a man, primarily because it weakens the entire relationship with his significant other. These kinds of insults can be scary to a man, primarily because within the dating and relationship economy, the male tends to be less valuable than the woman. In the current way that romance in America works, it is the expectation of the man to find the woman and not vice versa. Even as things continue to advance in terms of equality, this still remains to be the case for most relationships.

What this means for the man is that he will naturally be forced to compete with more men for the affections and attention of a woman, than the woman will be forced to compete with other women. Indicating that you have settled for him or that you could have better luck in a different relationship without really meaning it is a terrifying experience because of the sheer amount of energy that is required for a man to find another woman. In other words, it is easier for a girl to find a guy than it is for a guy to find a girl due to the competitive nature of the male world. This might seem like a generalization, but ask most men who they think has it easier. They will never say the woman.

Ultimately, a man needs to feel respect in order to function properly within a relationship.

When he doesn't feel that respect, he will begin to become destructive, either internally or externally. The most classic form of external destruction would be the explosive anger or shouting. The most common form of internal destruction is withdrawing from the conversation entirely, or as we would know it to be: shutting down. Why do men shut down and how can you get past that wall? Let's move onto the next chapter to find out!

Chapter 6: Getting Past The Stone Wall

If you've been in any kind of relationship with a man, you might notice that they tend to be the ones who are willing to disengage with the conversation when they begin to feel uncomfortable. Either they will change the subject, stop talking entirely or just blanketly agree with you in order to be maintain the peace. If you're trying to talk about something important, you will most likely experience a greater amount of agitation and you might even be tempted to get into a fight. Sometimes when you are fighting with him, you might realize that he has completely withdrawn.

We've already talked about one of the primary reasons why a man withdraws during a fight and that's because he is feeling disrespected which then leads him to feel wounded, but there are many other reasons why a man can pull away during a fight or a discussion. The better that you are able to understand the reason why he pulls away, the more you will be able to help him communicate what his thoughts and feelings are. So, what are some other reasons that a man shuts down during a discourse? Let's take a look;

Shutdown Reason One: He doesn't know how to solve the problem

Men are actionable creatures. One of the most common differences between men and women is the fact that men tend to look at things through an action lens. This means that when a man encounters a problem, his first inclination is to the solve the problem. It means that his instincts are to find the fastest and most practical solution to just about any issue facing in his direction.

Women are a little different in the fact that they would prefer to express and process their emotions about the problem, then figure out how to fix it. They aren't necessarily looking for a solution when they begin to communicate about a problem. This leads to one of the more classic communications between men and women, where a woman wants to communicate about the problem, as opposed to the man who would like to solve it. This inequality in communication will often lead to agitation between both parties, as the man will be frustrated that the woman isn't taking his advice and the woman will be irritated that she isn't really be listened to, but is instead trying to be fixed.

If just about every man approaches a problem with the intention of fixing it, what is he supposed to do when he is unable to solve it? When the problem becomes too great or when it seems unsolvable to him, he will react to the problem adversely. Either he will grow irate with the problem or he will feel an inadequacy since he can't fix it and pull back. This is usually one of the more common situations when it comes to dealing with an argument.

Sometimes a relationship issue can appear to be very overwhelming for a man. He doesn't look at problems as a matter of expression, but rather wants to focus on the solution. If the fight is about a serious disagreement, the man will try to figure out how to fix it, but usually the relational disagreements between men and women aren't about finding solutions but are rather about expression for the woman. This leads him to being overwhelmed and shutting down because he cannot find an obvious way to fix the issue.

This is a serious problem that plagues a ton of relationships. If you are looking to navigate through problems effectively, then you must be able to communicate to your man that he doesn't necessarily need to solve the problem at hand. Instead, try focusing on using statements about how you feel, and highlight your own emotions instead of trying to talk about the entire problem as a whole. Look at the difference between "You never listen to me!" and

"I feel that you don't listen to me." The second one is easier to understand because it clearly communicates a feeling. The first example communicates a problem. Communicating your own feelings helps reduce anxiety in the disagreement because he will be able to understand that the goal isn't to fix the problem, but rather to allow you to express yourself to him.

Shutdown Reason Two: He doesn't know what he's feeling

This is another common issue. As we've extensively looked at before, men aren't taught how to connect to their emotions or handle them properly. The masculine culture is relatively toxic and tells a man to suck it up and not feel anything, making it nearly impossible for him to be able to understand his more intense emotions. When he is in the middle of an argument or disagreement and he begins to feel sorrow, anger, dismay or disappointment, he might not be able to readily connect to those emotions and he might not have the ability to sort through them as effectively as a woman can. Instead of trying to slow things down and sort through the feelings, talking each one out, it is very easy for him to instead try to push his emotions down entirely. This will lead him to disconnect from the conversation entirely.

This is a tricky problem to deal with, because on the outside, all shutdowns tend to look exactly the same. The man stops talking, he draws back, he physically closes off his body language or worse, he leaves the room. It can be hard to tell what kind of shut down he is experiencing at any given moment. This is why it's important for you to be somewhat of a referee when it comes to handling arguments. You need to be able to monitor what his expression is and make sure that you don't push him too hard when you begin to disagree with him.

Of course, when you are emotional, this can be extremely difficult to do, as you will feel a greater level of impetus to fight due to your emotional charge, so it might be better to just cool down before you get into a greater discussion. Once the man has put up his wall, there really is no getting past it. You've got to be willing to work around this emotional disconnection and talk through it when he isn't feeling a surge of emotions that he doesn't particularly understand.

Shutdown Reason Three: He thinks he cannot win

This one is a tough one. Unlike the unsolvable problem, this isn't about a man's willingness to engage in the situation, but rather about his belief that an argument or a discussion will ultimately end up bad for him. Instead of wanting to work the problem out, he will give into the idea that it would be a fool's errand to try to win. This line of thinking is common in most relationships, because problem solving in a great deal of relationships is more about fixing the other person than focusing on finding ways to overcome what is at hand.

Look at it like this, if a man and a wife are in the middle of the argument about some kind of problem that he is causing, he will most likely feel that the wife is accusing *him* of being the problem. He won't realize that she is unhappy with the behavior, but instead will focus on her dissatisfaction with him. He will stubbornly conclude that he doesn't want to change *who he is* instead of focusing on changing what he is doing. So, since he doesn't want to change who he is, and since he thinks the problem is focused on him, he will realize that there is no way to solve the problem without changing. He views changing himself as losing. After all, who wants to become someone else? Since he doesn't want to lose, he won't engage in the conversation and then everyone loses.

The solution to this problem is to learn how to communicate that behavior is the issue. Don't say sweeping generalizations or use absolutes, such as always or never, instead try to focus on the problem at hand by clearing defining what the problems are. Try to angle the problem as something that both of you are facing instead of something that you are the only one who dislikes the behavior or actions. When you focus on the problem as independent of either party, you are increasing the chances of drawing him out and not causing him to shut down by making him feel like he is going to lose.

Another hard truth that a woman might have to come to terms with is the fact that a man's reticence to get involved in an argument or disagreement might have come from experience with her. He might have started out the relationship willing to emotionally engage in fights and disagreements, but learned that she never backs down from her original position. In that case, he learns rather quickly that he will never be able to compromise with her and wisely makes the decision to stop engaging. If this is the case, that his giving up during conflict is a learned behavior, then the woman is going to need to learn how to compromise and not always get the last word in. She cannot have it both ways, either she is willing to compromise and cooperate to solve the problem, or she can always be right and watch as her male relationships continually emotionally pull back and stonewall her for the rest of her life. She cannot have an emotionally cooperative man who is going to agree with her every single time. It's just impossible.

Shutdown Reason Four: His values are different

Sometimes a shutdown can happen simply because you two have different values. For example, if you are upset about him leaving the towels on the floor in the bathroom, he might not care at all about the problem. You may regard him leaving the towels as insensitive, rude and piggish, but he most likely isn't thinking about it at all. When you try to bring it up to resolve it, since his values are different than yours, he might come off as uncaring or distant. The reality is that this problem just simply isn't a problem to him. If he wanted to pick up the towels or was doing laundry, he'd do so without a problem. However, if you were to confront him about it, he might even be amused at your frustration.

This is another extremely common reason why there appears to be a male shutdown during the confrontation. Fortunately, this doesn't come from any serious emotional stuntedness, but rather it comes from a lack of understanding of values. The way to solve this problem is to communicate *how* something is important to you, instead of assuming that he considers it to be just as important. See, since you judge a specific action to be important to you, you will assume that neglect is involved when your man doesn't follow through with that specific action. However, if he doesn't deem it as important, then it isn't neglect at all.

By learning how to communicate why you feel something is important and how it makes you feel, you have a better chance of helping him understand your values. Once he understands what your values are, if he is someone who cares truly about you, he will begin to value them because he values you. Therefore, he would be willing to pick up the towels, not because he cares about picking them up but because he cares about you.

On the flipside, if you tried to push him into just blindly doing it because you said so, he would resent you and grow frustrated with you. It wouldn't be an act of love or service, but rather it would be an act of submission and most men don't care to be the submissive individuals in the relationship. Any relationship should be an equal partnership between both individuals.

Shutdown Reason Five: He doesn't want to hurt you

Male anger can crop up pretty quickly during a disagreement or a fight. Men are traditionally taught to suppress all emotions, all of them except for anger. Anger has traditionally been seen as the more masculine trait, so this means that it is perfectly acceptable for a man to grow angry during the course of a discussion. Of course, there is nothing wrong with anger, but how we display anger is important too. When it comes to disagreements, it's never okay to explode, scream, throw things or threaten to hit, but a man can feel all of these primal frustrations moving through him. He might have an instinct to say hurtful things, to smash things, to yell and scream, depending on how intense his emotions are running through him.

Of course, there are a lot of problems when it comes to expressing anger through action instead of words. The first is that it can be a genuinely terrifying thing for a woman to experience the physical rage of a man. The second problem is that things can never be unsaid. A man could lose his temper, smash a few plates and then say things he has no ability to take back. Most men do not want to be in this situation for a variety of reasons, the biggest is that they genuinely care about their partner and don't want to hurt them.

The fear of hurting his partner can quickly cause a man to shut down and refuse to continue talking or retreat from the location. From the woman's perspective, this might seem as if it were inappropriate and rude, but truthfully it is being done as a way to protect the woman from anger or malice. Ultimately, this exists because men aren't traditionally taught how to express their anger in healthy ways and instead know that it is far better for them to just pull back and not say anything rude at all.

So how can you solve this communication issue? Truthfully, the only way to solve this problem is to allow him sufficient time to cool off and try to communicate later on a healthier level. Don't focus on getting the last word in, or worse, don't follow him and try to continue the argument. His desire to move away stems from a need to calm down and take a breather, following him will only cause things to escalate to an even higher level.

Once the boiling point for a man has been reached, only time and distance will cool it down. There is no way that you can fix it, so don't try. This might seem a little fatalistic, but rather it is about being practical. Once you have caused an emotional argument to reach a point where he is angry enough to make rash decisions or lose control, you both have lost the argument. Try later when he has calmed down and things will be a lot easier. If you are finding out that this is reoccurring, it is probably a problem with both of your communication styles and you will most likely need to go to a professional couple's counselor in order to be able to figure out how to overcome these situations in the future.

Shutdown Reason Six: He believes conflict is bad

This is inherent in a lot of men who grew up in broken homes or homes that involved serious amounts of argument and conflict. He might have grown up to believe that conflict was a bad thing and something to avoid. The problem here is that there is no growth without any kind of conflict. Most people learn that conflict is necessary if they want to go somewhere in their romantic or professional lives, but there are a great many men out there who are content to just hang back and live life in the shadows instead of engaging in confrontation so that they can get what they want.

This can be troublesome when it comes to having conflict within a relationship. Truthfully, a good relationship doesn't necessarily need to be free of conflict in order to be good, but rather it needs to have a good amount of healthy conflict in order to be functional. Men who don't understand that conflict is a good thing will usually view any form of conflict as problematic and will do anything that he can in order to avoid it. This leads to either passivity or a cringe-inducing fear of fighting.

Passivity in a relationship looks like agreeability at first. You might think that he is simply always agreeing with you at first, but as things move along during the course of your relationship, you might find out that there are situations where he clearly disagrees with you, but he won't communicate that with you. Instead he will just try to change the subject or tell you to do whatever you want. This is evidence that his thinking is more about preserving peace and avoiding conflict than handling things that need handling. From the perspective of a woman who is trying to have equal, open communication, this can be extremely annoying.

Fear of fighting is similar to passivity, except that when conflict occurs, there is a total withdraw from the conversation. There isn't even an attempt to have dialogue about the conflict, but rather there is an adverse reaction from the man to the fighting itself. This stems from a destructive view of conflict and most likely comes from the fact that he has experienced conflict in the past and this conflict has left a bad impression on him. It might have come from family members always fighting, or a conflict with a prior relationship leading to disaster. Either way, when a man has a fear of conflict, it will essentially tank any chance of healthily resolving situations.

So how do you fix this problem if you are in a relationship with a man who fears conflict? Well, it isn't particularly easy, but you must work to convey to him that conflict is a good and valuable thing. You must be able to have a clear understanding of the nature of conflict so that you can explain it to him as well. If you have an aversion to conflict and he has an aversion to conflict, you two will never be able to sort through your differences. However, if you can help him see the value that conflict can provide and if you can exercise restraint while having conflicts with him, you two will be far better off.

Shutdown Reason Seven: Your pain is hurting him

Men are empathetic creatures, despite the fact that most of them don't have a great handle on understanding or dealing with their emotions. This empathy allows them to feel a great amount of love and sympathy for those who are in pain. When a man sees his woman in pain, he might actually begin to experience a sense of guilt and pain for what you are going through. Even if you aren't hurting because of his actions, the very presence of female tears and agony can create feelings of pain in him.

This might seem a little odd, but don't forget that men are biologically wired to protect. His defensive desires will flare up when he sees you in pain, but unlike the battlefield, there is no one to fight. This creates a feeling of helpless and even sorrow in a man. Some men react adversely to tears with fear, instead opting to become angry or frustrated that they can't solve the problem.

Yelling when you are crying might seem like the opposite of empathy, it might seem cruel, wrong and even evil, but it is the result of a deeply broken man who is unable to acknowledge how afraid he feels when he sees his woman feel pain. He might end up pulling away entirely because he feels shame at not being able to fix the problem. This will lead to nothing more than more sorrow and frustratiion on both parties ends.

So, what are you to do when you are working with a man who emotionally cannot handle the pain that comes from seeing you in pain? Well, it's not easy but you need to convey to him how he can help you just by listening. Don't try to hide your emotions, because that will only make things harder on you, but rather try to show him how he can assist you when you are in that fragile state. He has no idea how to handle it because no one has shown him. When left to his own devices, he will develop a coping method that frankly doesn't work well at all.

It's funny how communication is one of the most crucial things within a relationship, yet it tends to be the most neglected piece. This is partly because men haven't learned how to communicate effectively over the course of the last few thousand years. As we have seen, stonewalling is a result of a lack of being able to communicate during a disagreement, but what about during regular conversations? What about during the entire course of a relationship you are finding that your boyfriend or husband still cannot communicate properly? What do you do then? Let's move onto the final chapter to find out just how to communicate with men.

Chapter 7: True Communication

It's easy in the modern era to assume that all communication is the same. It's even easier, with all of the talk by the media about equality, to assume that men and women don't have any differences with the way they communicate. Truthfully, this couldn't be further from the truth. As we have seen, the male identity forms in a very unique and frankly, damaged manner, meaning that any communication that he engages in, will come from a damaged sense of identity. This isn't to mean that all men are broken and need to be fixed, but the truth is that most males struggle with communication because they weren't really taught what it means to communicate.

This last chapter is going to be focusing on learning how you can communicate effectively with men, so that you can do more than just simply resolve problems between you two, but also get to the place that you want to be in your own relationship. It is very easy for lack of proper communication to screw up any kind of relationship. If you believe that you are communicating properly and he isn't responding right, you might grow very agitated with him. It might lead you to become contentious or despondent, feeling that he doesn't care. Truthfully, it is entirely up to you to learn how to communicate the right way with a man, just as it's the man's responsibility to communicate the right way to you. Unfortunately, when it comes to these types of situations, someone has to be willing to make the first step. In an ideal world, it would be the man to make steps towards fixing these communication problems, but we don't live in an ideal world, so go ahead and roll your sleeves up. It's time to work on our communication skills with men!

Communication Tip One: Be direct

Believe it or not, but men are very aware when they are dealing with you. They can tell when you are upset, frustrated, angry or sad. However, you might be hoping that they will pry enough to where you can then convey your own emotions to him, but most men aren't like that. Most men, when they are told "oh it's nothing," or "I don't want to talk about it," will take this at face value because they are used to communicating clearly with other men. When a man wants something, he will often just say it. He doesn't continually worry about how he will say it or how it comes off, instead he just directly approaches the situation and says what he needs to say.

Women, on the other hand, tend to be more drawn back about communicating. They aren't as direct as men and tend to take a while to warm up to express themselves. This can be extremely frustrating for a man, primarily because he is used to just saying what he's thinking. He doesn't worry about his moods and when he communicates, he is extremely direct. When he sees, a woman trying to communicate indirectly, it can actually irritate him because he will perceive it as some kind of game playing. Your intentions might be perfectly pure, but if he senses there is more going on and you're not telling him, he will feel frustrated. Instead of trying to pry and see what he can learn, instead, he will just draw back and be content to allow you to communicate whenever you feel like it.

If you want to have a good relationship where information freely moves between both sides, then you are going to have to make a point to clearly communicate your intentions. Instead of being vague or worried what he thinks when you express yourself, just be honest. Say what you mean and mean what you say. When you are able to communicate clearly and without hiding behind generic phrases, you will find that he will be far more responsive and understanding than you would have guessed.

Communication Tip Two: Avoid Multi-tasking

What's interesting about the male brain is that it is a highly-focused machine, but it's usually designed to focus on only one task at a time. When he is engaged in something like working, gaming or building something, his mind will be entirely engaged in it. Women, on the other hand, tend to be far better at multitasking and in the process, can do multiple things at once. They can spend time on the phone, clean, cook and plan their week pretty much all at the same time. Men aren't nearly as capable of multitasking as that.

What creates a tension within communication is when a woman tries to get the attention of man whose mind is completely absorbed into something. For example, he might be working on his car when she asks him what he's planning for the weekend. He might grunt something back and go back to work or might end up ignoring her entirely. She'll feel frustrated at this and repeat her question, with a more agitated tone. He, still stuck in the repairing mode, doesn't answer again. Frustration rises in her and as she expresses that frustration, it begins to agitate him.

This plays out in plenty of relationships, primarily because women tend not to realize that men don't have the easy ability to move from subject to subject. They feel ignored, but in reality, the men just aren't able to switch gears so easily. If you want to learn how to communicate with men better, then you are going to need to respect the time that it takes for him to switch gears. He cannot really do two things at once. So, when he's watching television and you're trying to get his attention, instead of talking through his program and getting frustrated when he isn't responding to what you are saying, focus on getting his attention first.

The male mind works in gears. If his mind is entirely absorbed into the television show, it will take him a few moments to break away and refocus his concentration. Just like a car needs to shift gears when you are going from drive to reverse, a man needs to shift gears to a new line of thinking. If you shift to reverse without fully stopping your car, it's not very good for the transmission. It's the same with men, if you try to get him involved in a conversation when he's in the middle of something without giving him time to reset his focus and look at you, you'll just end up frustrating the both of you.

Just try to be patient and don't just rush into a conversation with him when he's distracted. Instead, signal to him that you want his attention and wait for him to shift gears. You might need to interrupt his focus and he might not particularly care for being pulled out of his mindset, but he won't be able to do two things at once, so you might as well save yourself a headache and get his undivided attention so you can tell him what you need to.

Communication Tip Three: Clearly communicate your needs

Similar to learning how to be direct, clearly communicating your needs can be a real godsend to men who are often considered to be clueless when it comes to relationships. The truth is that men aren't clueless, they just simply don't have the capacity to read minds. While it might be convenient and pleasant to have a man adequately able to guess what your needs are, that just won't really happen. It would be far better for you to clearly communicate what you need, as a way to eliminate guesswork.

When it comes to communication with men, guesswork is the absolute enemy. It creates anxiety, nervousness and above all, uncomfortableness. It creates reticence to engage in the situation. Clearly communicating to a man even the simple things can help the relationship move a lot more smoothly than you might think. For example, let's suppose that your birthday is coming up. Rather than just hope he remembers and get frustrated when he completely forgets, it would be far better if you were to tell him "My birthday is coming up soon!" Don't try to be negative and tell him "you better not forget my birthday like last year." because that isn't healthy communication. That kind of communication is toxic and guilt laden. He isn't obligated to celebrate your birthday, so turning it into an obligation will remove all of the joy from celebrating. Instead, just remind him if he's forgetful.

The way that men process information tends not to be based around what's most important, rather it tends to be focused on what is most present. If he has a lot going on in his life, if he's busy working, handling duties and going to school, he most likely won't remember things that are abstract concepts. Something like a birthday or anniversary is actually an abstract concept because it isn't in the here and now. Women tend to be better abstract thinkers, whereas men tend to deal more in concrete principles. If having him remember your birthday or anniversary is important to you, then you must be willing to invest the time into clearly communicating that to him.

The burden of communication is ultimately on the shoulders of the person who wants the better relationship. In an ideal world, both parties would shoulder the burden equally, but this simply won't happen. By stating each need that you have to him and clearly indicating when those needs are being fulfilled or when those needs are not being met, you are reducing the amount of guesswork in the relationship and freeing his mind up to focus on solving the needs that aren't being met.

Communication Tip Four: Get to the point

Keeping in mind the fact that men compartmentalize and process through things in a linear fashion, it's important to keep communication with him very direct and to the point. There can be an immense temptation to just begin unloading all of your information onto him, but since he's not able to multi-task, he won't be able to fully follow the information that is provided. The reason for this is because the information that a woman unloads tends to be interconnected at various points and doesn't work in a linear fashion.

For example, suppose a woman were asking her husband about what his availability is on Friday, she might say something like "Hey dear, I was talking with Susan the other day about where we're going to have dinner Friday night, and you know Italian is my favorite, so I was thinking that, but anyway, she told me she didn't care, and said that I should invite you along, and I said if she'd be okay with Italian food and she said that sounded good to her. Anyway, are you free for dinner with me and Susan on Friday?'

Now, that might seem like a relatively straight forward paragraph, but for most men, there are multiple stopping points for his mind to fixate on. The first stopping point in that above conversation was that fact that she was talking with Susan. Now he's thinking about her. Then she progresses to talking about dinner, which he then begins to think about, but she abruptly changes subjects, mentioning that Italian is her favorite kind of food. Now, for a woman this might seem incredibly connected to the conversation, but for a man, it seems almost entirely out of place. His mind then struggles to follow with the relevancy of Italian food and then by the time that you've reached the request to invite him to dinner, he's completely lost. He hasn't had time to process through anything at all.

Suppose instead of saying that long, drawn out paragraph giving him a play by play, the wife were to simply say "Do you want to come to dinner with Susan and I on Friday? We're having Italian." Would that be a better and more direct way to converse? Men can't always keep up with the pace of conversations when topics are rapidly changing, primarily because of the way their brains function. If you're just making idle conversation, it's perfectly fine, but if you want to achieve some kind of result in your conversation, try to keep things as direct and to the point as possible. The faster you can get to the end conclusion, the less overloaded that he is going to feel in the long run.

Communication Tip Five: Ask, don't tell

When trying to achieve something specific, it can be very easy to fall into a pattern of simply just telling the man what you want him to do. But when you tell someone to do something, you are assuming a position of authority and command. This is no way for a relationship to exist, for if you are always dictating terms to a man, he will quickly grow to resent you. Instead of telling them what to do, just ask them to do it instead. When you ask a man to do something, it is a powerful sign of respect. When you just bark out an order or assume that he'll do it because it's his responsibility, you are violating that ever-important respect that he holds in high regard. The art of respecting a man means asking instead of telling, pretty much in any situation.

Communication Tip Six: Compliment him

Men function best when they feel that they are achieving greatness. The deep desire of their heart is to get stuff done and have real significance in this world. When in an interpersonal relationship, he craves to be told that he is a conqueror, that he is doing a good job, that you're proud of him and that you are happy with him. Be specific and you will find that it will empower him on a higher level than you might have thought.

This honestly works for both men and women. The world is a cruel place, full of disappointment, sorrow and disagreement. Most people aren't really told that they are doing well, that they are loved and how happy they make others. You honestly can't compliment someone enough and when you truly, lovingly encourage them, you can make all the difference in the world.

One thing that is important when complimenting men, however, is to learn how to compliment him in a meaningful way. Don't just say something generic like "you're such a good guy," those things are nice, but they don't really hit the heart of a man. If you want to encourage him and strengthen your communication, you must be willing to speak to his heart. If the heart and desire of a man is focused around achievement and getting things done, if his innermost desires are to be valid and be a hero, then try to compliment him in such a way that it speaks to that part of him. Instead of saying, "you look nice today," try saying, "you really know how to put an outfit together." Rather than say "you're a great man," you could say "no one else out there can do what you do and I'm so lucky to know you." These types of compliments don't stroke some superficiality, but instead speak to the very soul of the man.

Communication Tip Seven: Prevent Fault Distribution

When trying to communicate, assigning blame can immediately distance you from a man. When he feels like he is to blame, he will become defensive and if he's not in the mood for a fight, he will pull back. Now, if you want to have a quick conversation without him pulling back, you're going to have to learn to how to communicate about simple issues without assigning blame or inferring that he is to blame.

Blame can easily show up in something like "did you remember to grab the milk like I told you to?" This clearly communicates to him that he is going to be blamed for his failures to remember the milk. This can quickly cause defensiveness in him. Instead saying "did you grab the milk on the way home?" can elicit a much faster reply. Instead of trying to defend himself from you, he'll realize that he forgot and then figure out how to handle the problem from there.

Blame doesn't help anyone. A guy knows when he has messed up. Coming at him with accusations or pointing the finger at him will only further embarrass him when he has failed. No one likes to be kicked when they are down, so when you are trying to solve a problem or communicate about your needs, don't try to make him feel worse than he already does.

Communication Tip Eight: Don't bring up the past

Unless you are actively working on a problem that involves some past transgression, you should strongly consider the past to be considered off-limits during a discussion. Bringing up the past is unfair and causes undue stress on the man when it is time to sort through something. It might be easy to tell him "Don't forget the milk, like you forgot yesterday," because that can sting. It is veiled criticism of him and it will sting. Yet this is something that is very easy to do. When you have resolved through a problem, log it away in your history files and forget about it. There is no reason to bring it up several days, weeks or even years later. It will only serve to cause more wounds in the long run.

Conclusion

The masculine mind is far from a simple machine. It is, in fact, just as confusing, wondrous, complex and interesting as the female mind. It is very easy in this modern era to listen to what the sitcoms, movies and gossip blogs tell us about the masculine soul, but in doing so, we are forgetting that men are equally as human as women. They are wired differently for sure, but we all have the same blood, the same needs and the same kinds of desires. Their needs just manifest in a different way.

As you have seen in the course of this book, the state of manhood is in a constant state of peril due to the fact that men have progressively been losing their sense of identity. The more blurred the lines between gender become, the more that progressives push not only for equality but also for stripping away the uniqueness of each gender, the more men will lose their sense of purpose. This loss of purpose will only continue to lead to the decline of quality within the male world. Women are excelling better than ever and with each passing day, they continue to break more and more ground. Yet, we cannot leave men behind, nor can we assume that they will get along just fine. We must continue to push for a greater presence of fatherhood in the lives of the young boys who exist in this world. We must, together, work so that both genders can flourish equally. It won't be easy, but it is possible.

We hope that by reading this book that you have a better understanding of what is going on within the heart, soul and mind of a man and that you are able to communicate with him more easily. Remember, men are wired to achieve, their hearts and minds are obsessed with doing great things. If you want to communicate to man properly, you must speak language of honesty, directness and action. For that is how you capture his heart and his attention. That is how you have true Manderstanding.

Other books available by Landon T. Smith on Kindle, paperback and audio:

Why NLP Isn't Working For You

The Art of Influence

The Power of Reflection: Embrace Your Past to Find a Purpose for Your Future

Meet Maslow: How Understanding the Priorities of Those Around Us Can Lead to Harmony and I